Animals Growing Up™

How Chimpanzees Grow Up

Linda Bozzo

Enslow Publishing
101 W. 23rd Street
Suite 240
New York, NY 10011
USA
enslow.com

WORDS TO KNOW

ape An animal, such as a chimpanzee, that has strong arms and no tail.

bond A close relationship with someone.

communicate To share information.

diet The kind of food an animal usually eats.

endangered In danger of dying out.

groom To clean an animal's skin and hair.

insects Small animals with six legs and a body with three parts that may also have wings.

predators Animals that kill and eat other animals to live.

skills Things an animal needs to know to survive.

CONTENTS

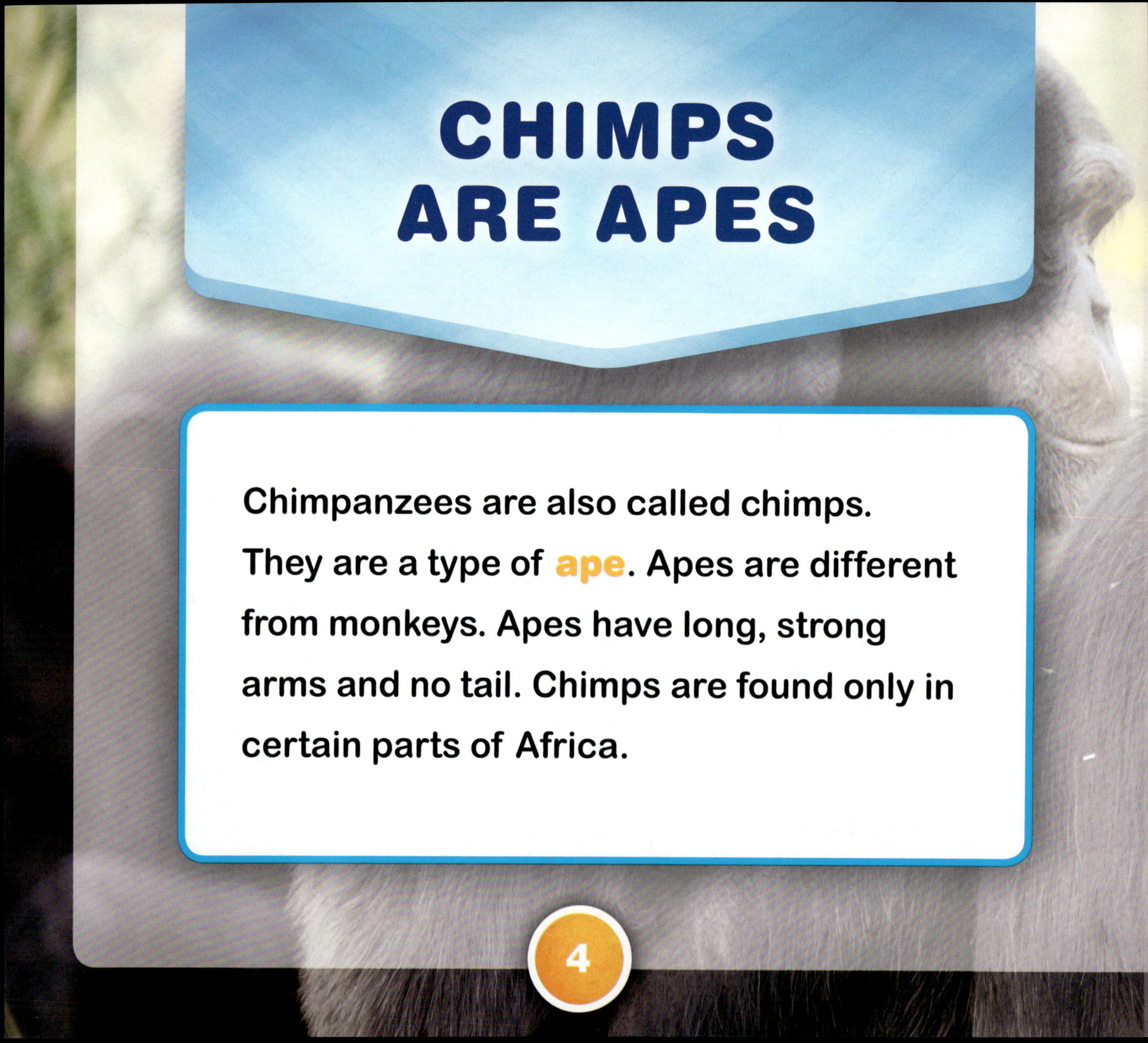

CHIMPS ARE APES

Chimpanzees are also called chimps. They are a type of **ape**. Apes are different from monkeys. Apes have long, strong arms and no tail. Chimps are found only in certain parts of Africa.

FAST FACT

Chimps are closely related to humans.

This chimpanzee mother is holding her baby.

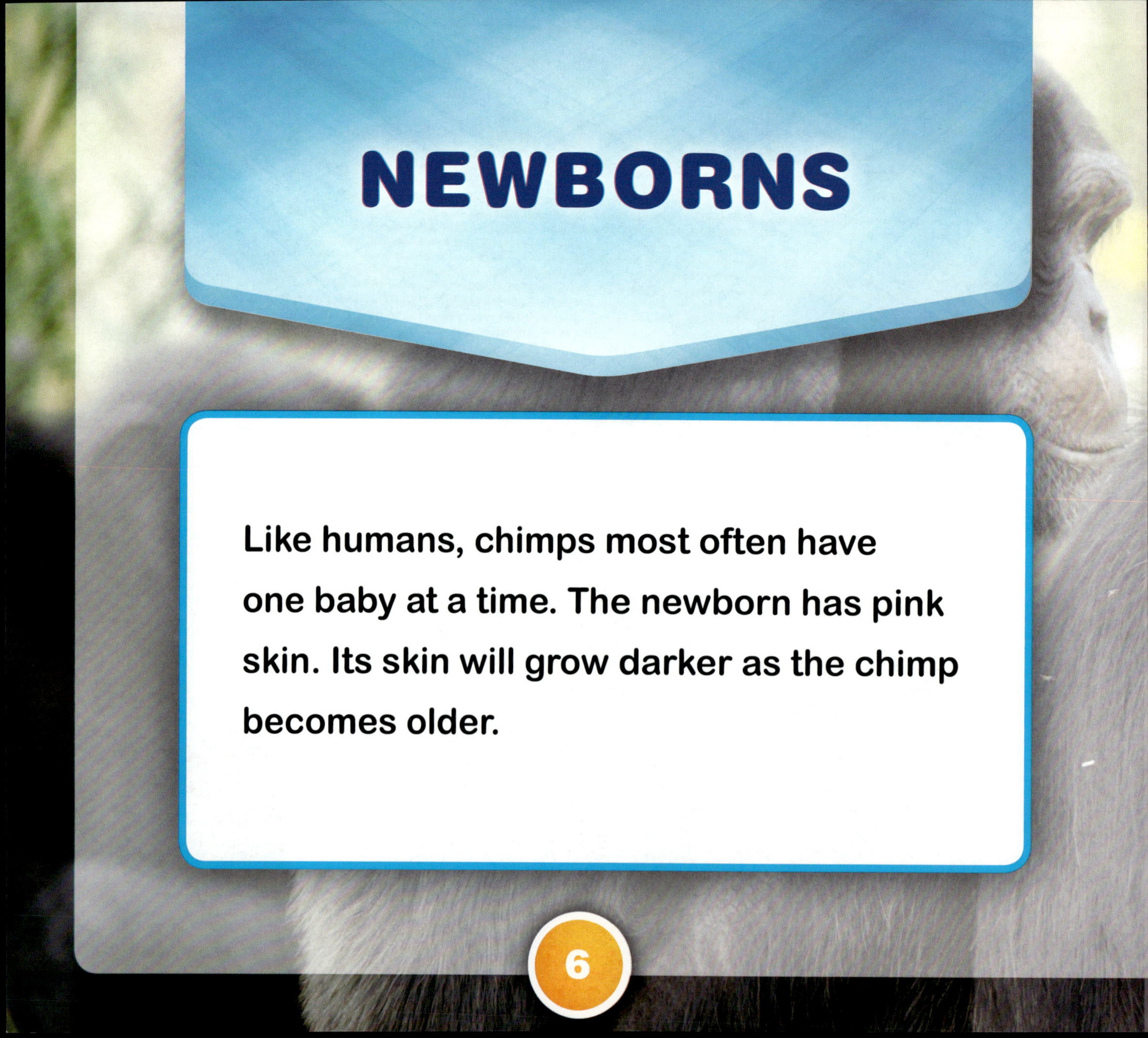

NEWBORNS

Like humans, chimps most often have one baby at a time. The newborn has pink skin. Its skin will grow darker as the chimp becomes older.

This baby chimp looks out from a tree in Africa.

FAST FACT

A white patch of hair near its bottom means the chimp is young.

BUILDING A NEST

Mothers build nests large enough for themselves and their babies. Nests are high up in trees to keep them safe from **predators**. These nests are made using branches and are very strong.

FAST FACT

Chimps do not like to sleep in the same nest more than once.

Chimp families rest in their nests together.

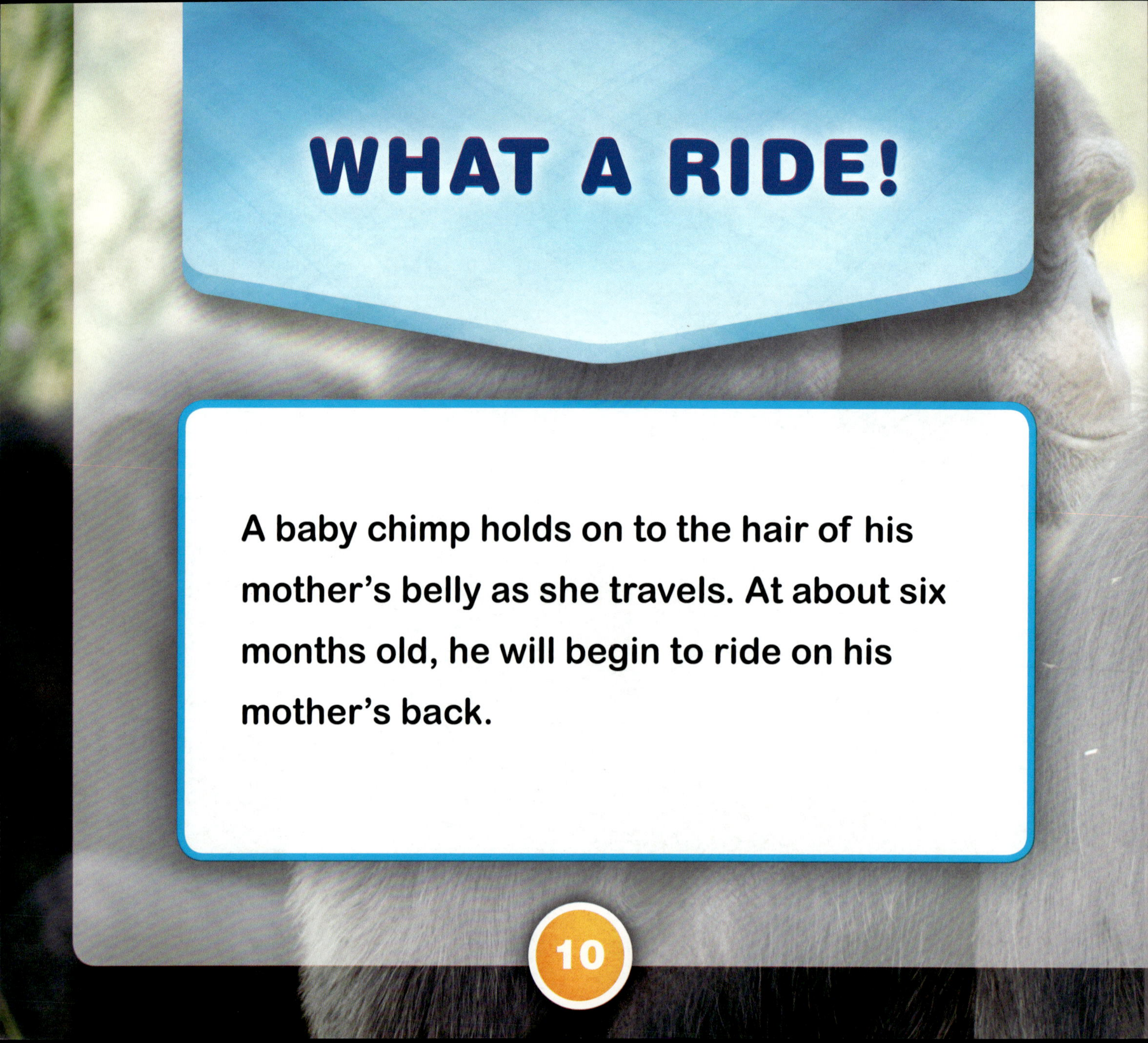

WHAT A RIDE!

A baby chimp holds on to the hair of his mother's belly as she travels. At about six months old, he will begin to ride on his mother's back.

FAST FACT

A young chimp travels on his mother's back until around the age of four.

A chimp is helpless at birth and needs its mother to get around.

SAFE EATING

Baby chimps will drink milk from their mothers for about five years. Their **diet** is mainly fruits. They also enjoy nuts, plants, **insects**, and meat.

FAST FACT

Baby chimps learn which foods are safe to eat by watching adult chimps.

This baby is two and a half weeks old. It drinks milk from its mother.

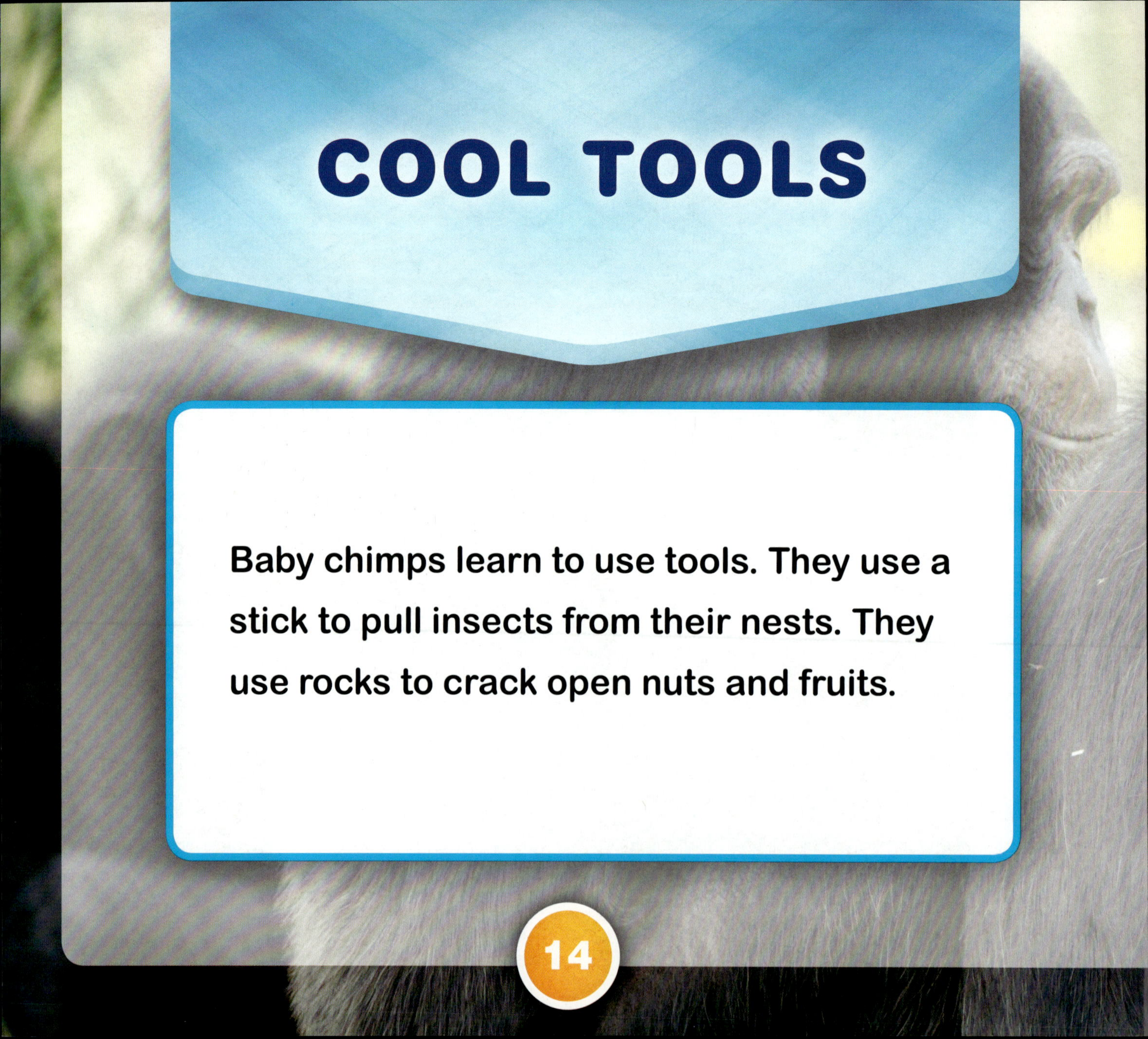

COOL TOOLS

Baby chimps learn to use tools. They use a stick to pull insects from their nests. They use rocks to crack open nuts and fruits.

FAST FACT

Chimps use more tools to help them get things done than any other creatures except humans.

A baby chimp can dip a stick into insect nests to get the bugs out. Insects are a tasty snack.

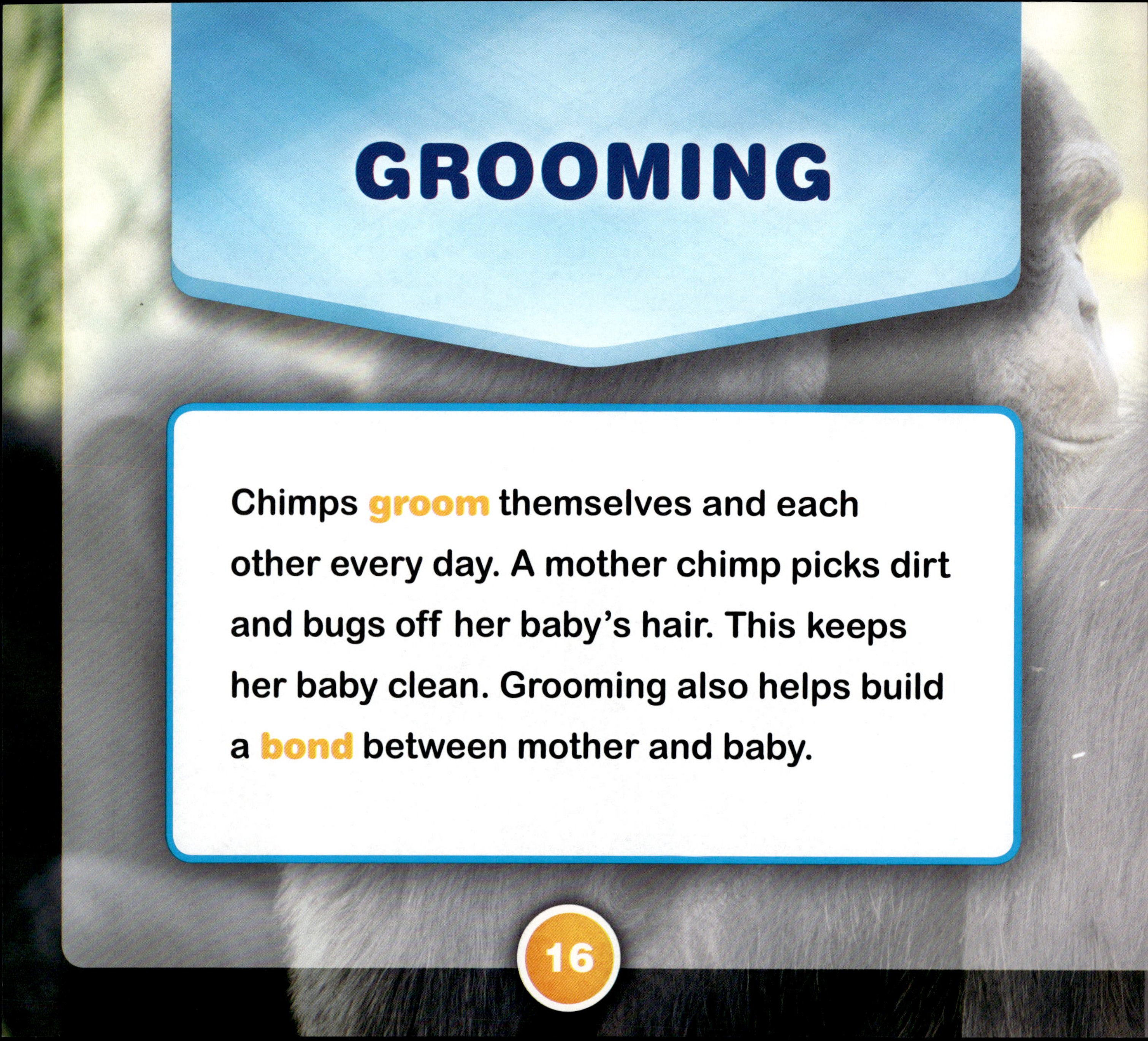

GROOMING

Chimps **groom** themselves and each other every day. A mother chimp picks dirt and bugs off her baby's hair. This keeps her baby clean. Grooming also helps build a **bond** between mother and baby.

FAST FACT

Chimps do not have hair on their faces, hands, or feet.

This mother is grooming her baby. It makes them feel closer to each other.

A LOVE FOR PLAY

Baby chimps love to play. They wrestle and chase each other up trees. They learn to **communicate** with each other through play. Playing helps them practice **skills** they will need as adults.

Young chimps wrestle with each other to build up their fighting skills.

FAST FACT

Chimps make sounds called play-pants when they are having fun. It looks and sounds like laughing!

KEEPING SAFE

A mother chimp cares for her baby alone. The father chimp does not help care for his babies. The mother guards her young from predators such as leopards.

FAST FACT

If something happens to the mother, a related chimp will take care of the baby.

Mother chimps watch over their babies to keep them safe as they grow.

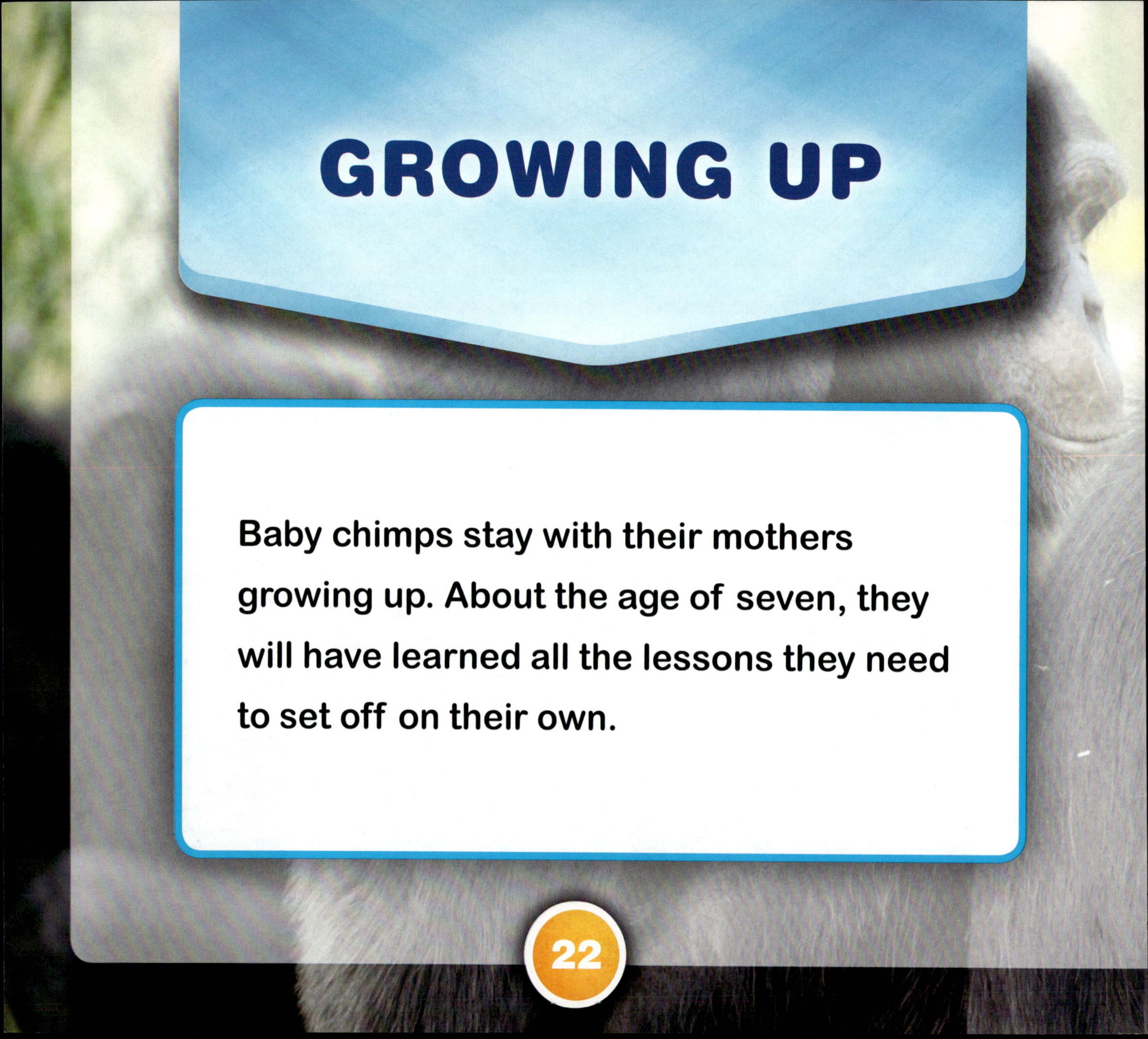

GROWING UP

Baby chimps stay with their mothers growing up. About the age of seven, they will have learned all the lessons they need to set off on their own.

A young chimp hugs its mother. Soon it will be on its own in the wild.

FAST FACT

In the wild, chimps are **endangered**. This means there are very few chimps left.

LEARN MORE

Books

Clay, Kathryn. *Chimpanzees.* North Mankato, MN: Pebble Books, 2019.

Grack, Rachel. *Chimpanzees.* Minneapolis, MN: Bellwether Media, 2019.

Kenan, Tessa. *It's a Chimpanzee!* Minneapolis, MN: Lerner Publications, 2017.

Websites

Easy Science for Kids: All About Chimpanzees
easyscienceforkids.com/all-about-chimpanzees/
Learn more about chimpanzees.

National Geographic Kids: Chimpanzees
kids.nationalgeographic.com/animals/chimpanzee
Read more about the lives of wild chimpanzees.

INDEX

Published in 2020 by Enslow Publishing, LLC
101 W. 23rd Street, Suite 240, New York, NY 10011

Library of Congress Cataloging-in-Publication Data

Names: Bozzo, Linda, author.
Title: How chimpanzees grow up / Linda Bozzo.
Description: New York : Enslow Publishing, 2020. | Series: Animals growing up | Includes bibliographical references and index. | Audience: K to Grade 3.
Identifiers: LCCN 2019001968| ISBN 9781978512276 (library bound) | ISBN 9781978512252 (paperback) | ISBN 9781978512269 (6 pack)
Subjects: LCSH: Chimpanzees—Development—Juvenile literature. | Chimpanzees—Infancy—Juvenile literature.
Classification: LCC QL737.P94 B69 2020 | DDC 599.88513/92—dc23
LC record available at https://lccn.loc.gov/2019001968

Printed in the United States of America

To Our Readers: We have done our best to make sure all website addresses in this book were active and appropriate when we went to press. However, the author and the publisher have no control over and assume no liability for the material available on those websites or on any websites they may link to. Any comments or suggestions can be sent by email to customerservice@enslow.com.

Photos Credits: Cover, p. 1 Cuson/Shutterstock.com; interior pages 4–23 (background), p. 5 barmalini/Shutterstock.com; p. 7 Gudkov Andrey/Shutterstock.com; p. 9 Danita Delimont/Alamy Stock Photo; p. 11 dmvphotos/Shutterstock.com; p. 13 © iStockphoto.com/Liz Bridges; p. 15 The Sydney Morning Herald/Fairfax Media/Getty Images; p. 17 Daryl Balfour/Getty Images; p. 19 Picture by Tambako the Jaguar/Moment/Getty Images; p. 21 Kristof Degreef/Shutterstock.com; p. 23 atiger/Shutterstock.com; back cover and additional interior pages background graphic 13Imagery/Shutterstock.com.